250
Big Ideas
for Purpose Driven® Small Groups

By Pastor Steve Gladen and Pastor Lance Witt

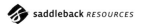

30021 Comercio
Rancho Santa Margarita, CA 92688
www.saddlebackresources.com

The phrase **Purpose Driven**® is a registered trademark of PurposeDriven® Ministries.
All rights reserved.

Dedicated
to the faithful
Small Group Leaders
of Saddleback Church
Lake Forest, California

ACKNOWLEDGMENTS

Effective small groups are a team effort. So are books!

We are grateful to the many small group leaders who tirelessly seek to live out God's purposes in the context of community, and to the crew of Area Leaders and Community Leaders who know the challenges, blessings, and growth that come in small groups.

We would also like to thank the Membership Team and Maturity Team at Saddleback Church, Purpose Driven Ministries, and Tim Smith for their remarkable resourcefulness, creativity, and commitment to the vision.

Our thanks to Jeanine and Dawn, who kept us on task and organized.

And special thanks to our supportive wives, Lisa and Connie, who give us grace when we need it most!

TABLE OF CONTENTS

INTRODUCTION

It's two hours before your group will meet. You need something to get the group going, but you do not have a lot of time or creative energy . . .

WHAT DO YOU DO?

The group members do not seem as close or connected as they used to be . . .

WHAT DO YOU DO?

At times the Bible study you do together gets a little too routine . . .

WHAT DO YOU DO?

Your small group wants to minister to other believers in a special way . . .

WHAT DO YOU DO?

"Evangelism" isn't in your group's vocabulary, and "missions" is a foreign word to your group . . .

WHAT DO YOU DO?

Your small group really wants to worship together . . .

WHAT DO YOU DO?

WHAT DO YOU DO?

You use ***250 Big Ideas for Purpose Driven Small Groups***.
Designed *by* experienced small group leaders *for* small
group leaders, this book offers 50 ideas for each of the
five purposes of a small group:

 FELLOWSHIP (Creating true community)

 DISCIPLESHIP (Cultivating spirituality)

 MINISTRY (Caring for each other)

 EVANGELISM (Communicating Christ to the world)

 WORSHIP (Celebrating our Lord)

We hope this little book impacts your small group in a
Big way.

Please write to us and let us know what works for your
small group!

> Steve and Lance
> Small Group Ministries
> c/o Saddleback Church
> 1 Saddleback Parkway
> Lake Forest, California 92630

FELLOWSHIP

FELLOWSHIP

Two's Company

Meet with another small group either from your church or another church. A shared Bible study like that can be a tool for Christian growth as well as an opportunity to establish fellowship with another group. Discuss with the other group any unique aspects of their meetings and glean ideas for new ways to approach your own Bible study time.

FELLOWSHIP

Warp Speed, Mr. Scott!

A day-long or an overnight group retreat can be a special time of fellowship. It is the same as a month's worth of group meetings, and is a great way to accelerate friendships within your small group.

FELLOWSHIP

Cookies

Pass around a tray of Oreos®, animal cookies, chocolate chip cookies, and vanilla wafers. As the tray goes around the circle, ask your group members to choose the cookie that best reflects their personality and explain why they chose their cookie. You can also ask them to demonstrate exactly how they eat the cookie. Don't forget to bring milk!

FELLOWSHIP

Valentine's Day Rescue

Have you noticed that it gets more and more difficult to be creative and romantic year after year? Let's help each other out! A few weeks before Valentine's Day, divide the men from the women in your group. Instruct each group to brainstorm ten creative ways to say, "I love you" to their spouse. Provide construction paper, markers, and scissors so that they make a valentine and incorporate one of the ideas the group generated. They could plan a surprise getaway or make a coupon for a romantic date: "This heart represents my never-ending love for you, and can be redeemed for one long walk on the beach followed by a double cappuccino." After Valentine's Day, have group members share their spouse's response to the special "I love you."

FELLOWSHIP

Group Ambush

Find out when and where another group from your church is meeting. Show up unannounced at the beginning of their meeting and explain, "You have been selected to be ambushed with love!" Unveil some treats you have brought for them, give a few hugs, and leave. Return to your usual meeting spot for some laughter, fellowship, and your own Bible study and prayer time.

FELLOWSHIP

Who Knew?

Ask group members to list five details about their lives that most people in the group may not know—be sure to do it too. Collect the papers for use at the next group meeting.

Before your next meeting, list some of these obscure details on a sheet of paper and make one copy for each group member. On your copy note which group member shared which fact.

When you meet again, pass out the sheets, saying, "Here are some of the facts written down last week. Next to each fact write the name of the group member you think shared it. You have three minutes."

When the time is up, read from your answer key. The person with the most right answers wins a "know-it-all" award (consider something fun like a $5 Starbucks® card). Give the person with the fewest correct answers a pack of name tags to help him/her get to know the group. ☺

FELLOWSHIP

Getting to Know You

Write some fun and easy-to-answer sharing questions on small pieces of paper (one for each group member including yourself). Tape a piece of paper under each member's chair before the meeting begins. Here are the kinds of questions you can use:

- Describe your favorite outfit when you were a teenager.
- What is the most annoying commercial on TV?
- What is your favorite chair in your house? Why?
- If you could learn one new skill this year, what would it be?

At sharing time, have each member retrieve the paper from under his or her chair. Then go around the circle and ask each person to answer the question on their paper.

FELLOWSHIP

Spice People

Bring out all the spices from the kitchen and place them on a table in the center of the group. Begin your group time by asking members, "Which one of these spices best represents you tonight—and why?" Be ready to get the discussion going by answering this question yourself.

FELLOWSHIP

Nerf® Sharing

Use a Nerf ball to encourage and even control sharing. Toss the ball to the person whose turn it is to share. When that person has finished, he/she chooses whom to hear from next by tossing the ball to that group member. This ball can also help you control talkative people in your group. Simply establish and enforce The Nerf Rule: You can't talk unless you're holding the Nerf ball.

FELLOWSHIP

Group Call

Make a group telephone call from your meeting to any member who is absent. Pass the phone around so everyone can talk. Open the call by saying, "We just want you to know that we miss you. Here's Nancy . . ."

FELLOWSHIP

Life Graph

Pass out graph paper to the group members. Ask them to first make a timeline of their life along the bottom of the paper and then to indicate with a graph whether the events were high points, low points, or somewhere in between. Have each group member take a minute to share their "life line," holding it up for others to see.

FELLOWSHIP

Off the Wall

On a piece of butcher paper (at least 2'x3') write "Community is . . ." or "Something I would like to discuss in our small group is . . ." Hang the paper on a wall. Making sure you have pens that won't bleed through the paper onto the wall, ask members to finish the sentence you began. Use their answers to fuel a brief discussion or give you ideas for future meetings.

FELLOWSHIP

Straw Draw

Cut straws into different lengths. Hold them in your hand so they look about the same length. Then have group members draw straws. Ask the person with the shortest straw to respond to the sharing question first. The person with the next shortest straw will go next, and you'll end with the person with the longest straw. Here's an option to this plan: let the person with the shortest straw decide who will answer the question next.

FELLOWSHIP

Road Trip

Find a road map. (Any state will do.) Not letting the members see which state you've chosen, read the names of obscure towns. See if people can guess which state—or, if you chose your own state, which county—you are looking at. Then ask group members where they are on their spiritual journey. Give them the following options and have them explain their choice:

- in the fields
- lost in the woods
- enjoying the country
- comfortable in the suburbs
- commuting, but missing out
- living in the Big City

FELLOWSHIP

Card Chat

Fold index cards in half so they stand up. On one face write a fun, creative question (e.g., "Describe your favorite childhood pet," "What was your wildest outfit as a child or teen?" or "What TV character are you most *not* like?"). Place these cards on the chairs or on a table in front of each seat. When people sit down, have them read their card and, if the group isn't too big, share their answer with everyone. If the group is large, have members share their answer with a person next to them. After they answer the first question, have members move two spots to the right and answer the question that is now in front of them.

FELLOWSHIP

Stick Family

To get to know about each group member's family, ask them to draw stick-figure pictures of the people in their family. On your sample, have Mom and Dad stand taller than the kids, who are arranged in a stair-step order. Ask members to write the people's names and add a simple graphic touch that reveals something unique about each person in the family. If the oldest daughter plays basketball, for instance, draw her holding a ball. Then have group members share their works of art.

FELLOWSHIP

Family Portrait

Don't worry if art isn't your thing! In one of your first meetings, have group members bring in a family photo so you can get to know each other's families. Give every person a minute or two to say something about each family member's interests, grade in school, or unique personality.

FELLOWSHIP

Who Wudda Thunk?

Have group members bring their wedding pictures to one of your meetings. Let each person talk a little about their wedding day and what is most unexpected about where they are today. If you have single people in your group, ask members to bring in a high-school or college yearbook, show their picture, and say whether high school or college was a high point or low point for them and one reason why.

FELLOWSHIP

The Newlywed Game

Take a break between studies and play *The Newlywed Game.* Make up the questions, get fun little prizes for the winning couple, and have a blast. Here are some questions to get you started!

Wives: What's your husband's favorite vacation spot for the two of you?

Where was your first meal together?

What is one thing your husband did recently to make you feel special?

Husbands: What was the color of the outfit your wife wore yesterday?

What would your wife say is your greatest area of growth in communicating? Listening, talking, resolving, or all of the above?

What would your wife consider more romantic; a picnic at the beach as the sun sets over the ocean, a candlelit dinner at home cooked by you, a surprise weekend getaway, or staying at home with you, ordering in pizza, and watching a good video?

Bonus Question: Who's the family expert at bodily function noises, him or her?

FELLOWSHIP

Cinco de Mayo

Sometime around May 5, have a potluck taco bar* and enjoy a fiesta dinner. Decorate with bright red, yellow, and green—and don't forget the piñata.

*Ask people to bring one or two of the following: cooked taco meat, taco shells, grated cheese, diced tomatoes, shredded lettuce, sour cream, salsa, avocados or guacamole, paper goods, and drinks.

FELLOWSHIP

Cyber Sharing

Communicate to group members via the Internet. Consider having a between-meeting newsletter that will keep people updated on each other's lives, remind people what to study, notify members of any details about the next meeting, report prayer requests and praises, and provide group members an opportunity to share news with other members. Cyber communication can also happen if those America Online types in your group are on each other's Buddy List, or if members set up instant messaging with each other.

FELLOWSHIP

Bent and Fuzzy

Pass out a pipe cleaner to each person. Ask group members to bend the pipe cleaner into the shape that best symbolizes or reflects their day or week. Take turns showing your pipe-cleaner creations and explaining the reason for your shapes.

FELLOWSHIP

Been There, Done That

Give each person ten small candies (Reese's Pieces®, M&M®'s, Skittles®, or Hershey's Kisses® work well). Go around the circle and have group members tell about something they have done or someplace they have been. The goal is to share an experience that no one else has had. Everyone who has not "been there, done that" must give the speaker one piece of candy. The game continues until most people run out of candy—or they start eating it!

FELLOWSHIP

It's Your Life!

Have group members share a brief account of their spiritual journey. These stories are a great way to get to know each other better. The stories can also prompt group members to extend compassion, patience, and love to one another.

FELLOWSHIP

So How Are You Doin'?

Ask one or two people to share how the Lord worked in their lives during the previous week. It is always inspiring to hear what God is doing in people's lives. These stories will encourage group members to consider how God is working in their own lives. These stories are just as important for the people in your group who are not yet believers. They need to know that God is active in our lives in very real, very personal ways.

FELLOWSHIP

What's in the Box?

Think of a different ice-breaker question for each member of the group. Write each question on a separate piece of paper. Fold the papers in half and put them in a box. At the group meeting ask members to take one paper from the box and answer the question. Here are some possible questions:

- What is one of your goals for this year?
- What is your favorite place for quiet time?
- What is your favorite restaurant and why?

FELLOWSHIP

From Far Away

Find some postcards from faraway places and use them to send group members a note of encouragement or a reminder of a special event. They'll be surprised to see that the exotic note is from someone in town!

FELLOWSHIP

Guys' Night/Girls' Night

Suggest that your group do a Guys' Night/Girls' Night. Once each month or two, the guys go out to dinner and the girls go out to dinner—at different restaurants. If children are in the picture, guys and gals could go out on different nights, and whoever doesn't dine out will hang out with the kids.

FELLOWSHIP

Prayers in a Bucket

Is it time for your group members to move to the next level of intimacy and transparency? If so, try this. Send home a small piece of paper with each person. Ask them to spend some time in prayer and then write down one hurt, a specific issue, or a particular burden they are struggling with—but don't write their name. Remind them to bring the paper back next week. As each person arrives, have them put their folded paper in a box or bucket. Before you start reading those pieces of paper, remind group members that the point is not to try to figure out who wrote what, but instead to help each of us let go of our burdens and hurts, to give them to God, and to pray for each other. Ask group members to close their eyes as you open in prayer. Then, one by one, read each prayer concern and pray about it. Close by thanking God that all these matters are in his sovereign and loving care.

FELLOWSHIP

Secret Road Trip!

Have your group plan to take a road trip together—either a visit across town, a day trip, or even a weekend getaway. Take turns planning trips. Remind people that the bigger the trip, the more planning required! Wherever you go, the time together in a car and the adventure of going to a destination that's probably new to some in the group will help strengthen fellowship.

FELLOWSHIP

Putting Out the Welcome Mat

Anytime someone new joins the group, go out to eat together. A casual restaurant is a comfortable, nonthreatening setting to introduce the new person to the group. It can sometimes be awkward for a new person to find himself sitting in a stranger's living room, surrounded by people he doesn't know. But a restaurant meeting, on the other hand, is just about having a meal, some laughs, and a good time.

A restaurant meeting is also great for inviting nonbelievers. It can be tough to invite a nonbelieving coworker to church and even tougher to invite him or her to a Bible study group. It's much easier to invite that coworker to a restaurant to have dinner with a bunch of your friends.

FELLOWSHIP

A Bible Connection

Want to help people find a book of the Bible they can really connect with? Bring in a Bible that has an interesting and well-written introduction to each book of the Bible. Have group members read the descriptions out loud. Ask each group member to listen carefully and, after all the intros have been read, choose one book they would like to get to know better. In subsequent weeks, ask members to share something they have learned in what just may be their new favorite book of the Bible!

FELLOWSHIP

"What You Bring to Our Group Is . . ."

Give each person a list of all the group members. Ask them to take the list home, spend some time in prayer, and then finish the sentence: "What you bring to our group is . . ." for each person listed. Remind the group members to bring the list with them to the next meeting.

At that meeting, go around the circle and have each of the group members read what they wrote about a particular person. Then go around the circle again for the next person listed. Repeat until everyone has been read to. It will be a great encouragement for each person to hear what a blessing he or she is to the other group members.

FELLOWSHIP

Game Night at Church

Divide the group into two teams, guys versus girls. Using a large easel and flip chart, play Hangman with names or words that only people at your church would know. You can do the same thing with Pictionary®. (It's always a blast to watch people draw their pastor!)

FELLOWSHIP

Year-End Reflections

Give each person in your group a slip of paper containing the statement, "For me, the greatest moment in our group this past year was . . ." Ask everyone to write their own ending to that sentence and to bring that slip of paper to your group's Christmas party. Give all the group members an opportunity at the party to share their thoughts and memories.

FELLOWSHIP

A Word of Encouragement

Have members of the group write and mail encouraging notes to each other. Give everyone a 3x5 or 4x6 index card. Help group members get started by writing on one side of the card the beginning of a sentence, something like "You are an important part of our group because . . ." Write the mailing address on the other side of the card.

FELLOWSHIP

Memories

Put together a scrapbook that traces the history of your small group. Include pictures of regular meetings as well as holiday parties, service projects, church events, and whatever else you've done together. The scrapbook is a great way to see how your group has grown and reached out to others. Be sure to review the book together anytime your group is about to give birth to a new group, or gathers with a group that had spun off earlier.

FELLOWSHIP

A Feelings Checklist

To gain some insight into your group members, ask, "What three emotions do you feel most often?" You may even find in their answers some opportunities to offer them spiritual and practical support.

Lists of options may help the conversation get started. Some positive feelings are blessed, calm, capable, confident, content, eager, friendly, gentle, lively, masterful, optimistic, outgoing, peaceful, and safe. Some negative feelings are afraid, alone, angry, anxious, bitter, discouraged, frantic, fuming, hurt, numb, scared, tense, uncomfortable, and worried.

FELLOWSHIP

Lights! Camera! Action!

Do you want to help your group move from discussion to action? As a first step, list those things your group wants to accomplish—spiritual goals for the group to tackle together, service projects to further God's kingdom on earth, or personal steps of growth they want to take. Put the goals down in writing, so that accountability and action can happen.

FELLOWSHIP

Got Milk?

In order to know your individual group members better and to enable them to know you, get together between meetings. Maybe have breakfast or lunch with a group member or two. Since everyone has to eat, mealtime is a great opportunity to get to know someone. If you're constrained by time or budget, meet for dessert, coffee, or a coke.

FELLOWSHIP

Know the Basics

Never tell anyone outside your group something that was shared in confidence by one of your group members. This basic small group rule may be common knowledge to you, but it's important for everyone in your group to understand and agree to the value of confidentiality. Nothing will destroy a group faster than gossip.

A good group exercise is to create a small group covenant or agreement that addresses issues such as:

- Shared group values (i.e., confidentiality, accountability, etc.)
- Shared responsibilities (i.e., snacks, tracking prayer requests, etc.)
- Start and stop times
- Informing the leader if you're going to miss a meeting
- How often the group will add new members
- Having written guidelines that everyone can understand and agree on can prevent conflict, enhance accountability, and strengthen your group's sense of identity.

FELLOWSHIP

More Than a Warm Fuzzy

Compliment a group member in front of the rest of the group. Besides affirming a group member (and that's very valuable!), you're also modeling one way for members to encourage each another. Try giving one genuine, heartfelt compliment to two people at each group meeting and watch the encouragement spread!

FELLOWSHIP

Touch Points

Always acknowledge your group members' birthdays and anniversaries. Be sure that when people come to your group, you not only get their name, address, and phone number, but you also get their birthday and anniversary (wedding and/or salvation). Save money by ordering birthday and anniversary cards in bulk from a card catalog. A card in the mail or on their seat when they arrive lets group members know that their special day is special to you!

FELLOWSHIP

Phone Tag

Call a member of your group when you know you can get an answering machine and leave an encouraging message. Be sure to remind that person that he or she is now "it." That person must call someone else in the group (not you!), leave a message on their answering machine, and tag that person "it." In your excitement to tag the next "it," remember to leave an encouraging message.

If you're playing Phone Tag on the day of a group meeting, you might raise the stakes and have the last person who is tagged "it" (approximately two hours before the small group meets) bring the snacks. That may be hard on the more organized folks in your group, though. One more thing: If not all of your group members have an answering machine, kindly tell those folks that . . . it's the twenty-first century!

FELLOWSHIP

And the Winner Is . . .

Give perfect attendance certificates or prizes to those members of your group who have made it to all the meetings in a set period of time. Besides appreciating these members' commitment, you're challenging others to follow their good example. You might also want to use this time to give some humorous awards for best snack, worst snack, group MVP, most likely to become a free agent, etc.

FELLOWSHIP

You've Got Mail!

E-mail group members to update them on group activities and to share a verse that has recently been meaningful to you. Let computer technology enable you to add a bit of joy and encouragement to the life of people in your group. If you or they do not have e-mail, send a note or postcard via snail mail. It's still mail—and it's still encouragement!

FELLOWSHIP

A Foundation for Success

Make sure your group members understand the commitment they're making and know what your expectations are. (For more help, see the resource on *"Deepening the Purposes in Your Group"* from PurposeDriven® Publishing.) Be their coach, their cheerleader, and their main support so they can experience the joy and blessings of small group membership.

FELLOWSHIP

Guess Who God Is Bringing Tonight?

Never cancel a meeting due to the number of people who might be absent. Remember that every single meeting is a divinely arranged appointment for you to minister God's grace and love to whomever he brings. If just a few people show up for your meeting, be sensitive to their needs. Don't hesitate to tailor your lesson and/or group time to the few who show up. Appreciate the opportunity that this smaller group gives you to get to know each other better.

FELLOWSHIP

A Change of Pace

During summer and the holidays, change your group's diet of weekly meetings. With everyone so busy, cut back on your regular meeting schedule a bit, but be sure to add some social events so you can enjoy the holiday or summer season together. Even when meetings are fewer, remember that people still need your care. We never take a break from shepherding our flocks.

FELLOWSHIP

Speak Truth in Love

When you have a problem with a group member—if the person is dominating conversations, if confidentiality has been betrayed, etc.—never confront that person in front of the other group members. Schedule some time alone outside of the group meeting, perhaps right before or right after your group time. Follow the Matthew 18 principle: Talk to that person first. If the problem persists, confront that person in the presence of another person. If the problem still persists, bring in a church official.

DISCIPLESHIP

DISCIPLESHIP

Book It

As you meet week after week, celebrate and encourage a group member in whom you see spiritual growth. Pull that person aside after a group meeting and present him or her with a copy of *The Pursuit of God* by A. W. Tozer. Be sure to write a personal note of encouragement and affirmation inside the front cover. (By the way, if you haven't read this book yourself, it is a *must* read.)

DISCIPLESHIP

A Spiritual Roadmap

Have group members talk about how they came to Christ as well as their spiritual journey since coming to Christ. Ask them to highlight the defining moments or key turning points along the way. You might plan to hear from two or three people each week for a month. Don't rush this exercise. It's a great way to get to know and better understand your group members.

DISCIPLESHIP

High-Impact People

Have group members talk about the person in their life who has had the greatest spiritual impact on them. Why was that person such an important influence? What was it about that person's character, words, or actions that sparked spiritual growth?

DISCIPLESHIP

Time for a Checkup

At least once a year, spend an entire meeting giving members the opportunity to assess their own spiritual health. Encourage honesty and authenticity. Ask each other, "Where are you strong and where do you need to grow?" Allow some time for members to work on an individual health plan and to map out a strategy for their spiritual growth.

DISCIPLESHIP

Top Ten List

Pass out a piece of paper to each person in the group. Have each person list the top ten qualities of a disciple of Jesus Christ. Ask people to share their answers with the group. Record the ideas on a piece of butcher paper that everyone can read, and see if you can reach consensus on the top ten.

DISCIPLESHIP

The TV Turnoff

Conduct a group experiment: Commit to turn off your TVs for one week. Encourage members to include their children in this exercise and to explain to them why they are doing this. Each day use one of the half hours you would normally spend in front of the TV to read the Bible or a classic Christian book. If you aren't sure which book to choose, ask one of your church leaders. At your next group meeting, take some time to discuss your experiences with living a "TV-less" lifestyle.

DISCIPLESHIP

The Devil Made Me Do It

How can temptation become a stepping stone instead of a stumbling block? Have a group—or two-group—discussion about this question regarding temptation. If you have both men and women in your group, you may want to divide into groups by gender so that people will feel greater freedom to talk honestly about the temptations they face.

DISCIPLESHIP

Garbage In, Garbage Out

Take a small garbage can to your group meeting and set it in the middle of the room. Then talk about the unhealthy thoughts, songs, movies, television shows, radio programs, books, magazines, etc., that we allow into our minds. Ask group members to write down those things God is calling them to stay away from. As people tear up the pieces of paper and throw them in the trash can, have them make a prayerful commitment to God to think on *"whatever is true, whatever is noble, whatever is right, whatever is pure, whatever is lovely, whatever is admirable— anything that is excellent or praiseworthy"* (Philippians 4:8).

DISCIPLESHIP

Be Quiet

Ask the entire group to read the same passage(s) during their daily quiet time this week. For example, you might consider having them read John 17 each day for five days. Encourage them to read slowly and to take notes on what they observe and what insights God gives them. The next time your group meets, read John 17, or your passage, out loud and ask people to share some of their thoughts with the group.

DISCIPLESHIP

Who Brought the Fertilizer?

Bring a plant to your group and set it in the middle of the room. Talk about the similarities between the growth and health of a plant and the growth and health of a Christian. Also ask, "Who is spiritual fertilizer for your growth? Who is it that makes you want to grow in your knowledge of the Bible, grow to become more like Christ, or grow in your Christian service in the world?" At the end of the group meeting, give the plant away to someone who has contributed to the growth of other group members.

DISCIPLESHIP

Tag-Team Scripture Memory

Put everyone's name in a hat or bowl. As you draw names, pair people up with one another. Give the whole group a Scripture verse to memorize over the next week. Ask people to check in with their partners throughout the week for practice and encouragement—and, yes, for accountability.

DISCIPLESHIP

Praying on Paper

Pass out a piece of paper to each person. Then have everyone read Psalm 96 individually. In the New Living Translation, verse 3 says, *"Publish his glorious deeds among the nations. Tell everyone about the amazing things he does."* Now have each person in the group write out a prayer thanking God for the "glorious deeds" he has done in their lives and the "amazing things" he does for them regularly. Ask for volunteers to read their prayers aloud.

DISCIPLESHIP

Walk in the Park

Plan a weekend group-walk through a park or along a nature trail. Decide on a time and location. Encourage group members to take along a Bible and even a lawn chair or blanket. When everyone arrives, instruct each person to go off separately and be alone with the Lord for an hour. When everyone returns to the meeting place, ask for volunteers to talk about their experiences. What did they realize about the value of this time? What did they sense God was saying to them? How hard was it to be quiet, and to focus on the Lord? How might this experience help you develop a regular quiet time?

DISCIPLESHIP

Sabbath Slowdown

Exodus 31:13 (NLT) says, *"Tell the people of Israel to keep my Sabbath day, for the Sabbath is a sign of the covenant between me and you forever. It helps you to remember that I am the Lord, who makes you holy."* As a group, talk about what it might look like to truly practice keeping the Sabbath in the twenty-first century. Remember the huge difference between grace and legalism!

DISCIPLESHIP

Take a Day Off

Set aside a specific Sunday for the whole group to practice the Sabbath. Let it be a day of total and God-focused rest. At the end of the day, gather for a relaxing meal—one with absolutely no agenda!

DISCIPLESHIP

Take Some Meditation Medication

One night during your group meeting, select a passage of Scripture—or simply turn to Psalm 1. Then let everyone sit quietly for twenty minutes to meditate on those verses. "Meditating" may sound scary or difficult. Explain to group members that they need only to read the passage slowly and prayerfully, making observations, asking what it reveals about God, and listening for what he might want to be teaching them right now. Group members may not find this exercise very easy. Acknowledge that fact, but encourage them to sit quietly with the passage and the Lord for the entire twenty minutes. Come back together and talk not only about the passage but also about the experience.

DISCIPLESHIP

The Fire of God

Have your group sit in front of the fireplace. While everyone gazes on the flames, read 1 Peter 1:7 (CEV). *"Your faith will be like gold that has been tested in a fire. And these trials will prove that your faith is worth much more than gold that can be destroyed. They will show that you will be given praise and honor and glory when Jesus Christ returns."* Ask people to share a time when they have been "through the fire." In what ways did these difficult times produce spiritual growth?

DISCIPLESHIP

Fast Forward

When Jesus taught about fasting in Matthew 6:16, he said "*when* you fast," not "*if* you fast." Decide as a group to do a one-day fast. This would mean giving up all food for a 24-hour period. Pray during those times when you would normally be eating. Also, choose a few situations that all of you will pray about during your fast.

DISCIPLESHIP

Spiritual Parents

Read 1 Thessalonians 2:7–12 and discuss the similarities between parenting and discipling. Ask the group, "Who, if anyone, has been like a spiritual parent to you? Describe the impact of that person on your life and faith."

DISCIPLESHIP

Unconditional Surrender

Read Joshua 24:1–27. Pass out a piece of paper to each person in the group. Then, just as the people of Israel made a covenant, have the group members write out a personal covenant describing their commitment to God. (It might be helpful to have people be alone with the Lord in different parts of the house.) After fifteen or twenty minutes, call the group back together and ask for volunteers who are willing to share their covenant. Encourage every group member to sign the covenant they wrote, date it, and keep it in their Bible to review from time to time.

DISCIPLESHIP

Stepping Stones

Read Joshua 3. Notice that the water didn't start to roll back until the priests stepped into the water. Only when they acted in faith and got their feet wet did they see God work. Have each person describe a time when, in faith, they had to step into the water. What situation demanded action and therefore stretched their faith—and what growth did that experience result in?

DISCIPLESHIP

Error Message

Here's a great homework assignment for group members to do with their families. Ask people to watch television for an evening and, as they do so, to list all the messages, implicit as well as explicit, in both programs and commercials, that run counter to the truth of God's Word. Encourage group members to point out and discuss these messages with their children.

Have group members bring their lists to the next meeting. As you talk about the items on the lists, specify the biblical truths they contradict. Then discuss what Christians can do to stand strong against these powerful and ever-present messages.

DISCIPLESHIP

Pick a Tune

At the close of a group meeting, give members the following assignment: In the coming week, find a song that describes your spiritual journey or reflects where you are now. Ask them to bring the CD and lyrics to the next group meeting. At that meeting, have people play their songs and explain why they selected that particular song.

DISCIPLESHIP

Favorite Scripture

A good way to get to know one another's faith stories is to ask people to identify a favorite verse or passage of Scripture. Ask them ahead of time to come to a certain meeting prepared to read their selection to the group and explain why that verse or passage is meaningful to them.

DISCIPLESHIP

Scripture Scavenger Hunt

Divide your group into two teams. Give the teams ten or fifteen minutes to find as many verses as they can about finances and stewardship—or about any other topic of special interest to them. Ask them to make a list of the verse references they find. The team with the most verses is the winner. Then, have each team read the verses or passages they found, and spend time asking people from both teams to share what they learned from their verses.

DISCIPLESHIP

Personal Retreat

At the beginning of the year, challenge every member to do a personal retreat, to set aside time (either a few hours or an entire day) for prayer and reflection. Encourage group members to first spend time thinking about the past few months: What has God been teaching them? What struggles have they faced? What prayers has God answered? Then have members spend time praying for God's direction and thinking about what he might be wanting them to do in the next few months. Out of this personal retreat should come some personal direction and goals for the coming months. Finally, ask members to let the group know when they plan to do their personal retreat. Have members write down these dates so they can hold one another accountable and pray for one another on those retreat days.

DISCIPLESHIP

Warm Fuzzies

Take time to affirm one another. Ask people in your group to share specific examples of the growth they have seen in fellow members. (You might let folks know this is coming ahead of time so that they can come prepared.) If you are the leader of the group, make certain that on the night of affirmation, no one goes unmentioned or unaffirmed. Close this exercise with a time of thanksgiving prayer for what God is doing in the lives of your group members.

DISCIPLESHIP

Take Note

Bring a variety of blank note cards to your group meeting. Have each person write a note of encouragement to someone outside the group in whom they have seen growth in Christ.

DISCIPLESHIP

A Word about the Word

In 1 Timothy 4:13 (NCV) Paul says, *"Until I come, continue to read the Scriptures to the people, strengthen them, and teach them."* Choose an evening to read Scripture aloud to one another. Select a book (you might try Philippians) and ask for different volunteers to each read an entire chapter to the group. Afterwards, talk about the experience of hearing God's Word and about how God spoke to you through it.

DISCIPLESHIP

The Jesus You Never Knew

At the end of a group meeting, challenge everyone in the group to read the book of Mark during the next week. Ask them to take notes in response to the question, "What did you learn about Jesus that you didn't know before?" Talk about their answers at the next meeting.

DISCIPLESHIP

Going Deeper

To help group members better appreciate the richness of Scripture, have them read and meditate on Philippians 2 every day this week. Ask them to write down one new thing they learn each day during these quiet times.

DISCIPLESHIP

Connecting with People of the Bible

Do you need a simple, nonthreatening way for folks to get to know each other? Ask the people in your group, "Who in the Bible do you most relate to? Why?" or "Who in the Bible, other than Jesus, would you most want to be like? Why?"

DISCIPLESHIP

Be Fruitful

Galatians 5:22–23 (NIV) says, *"But the fruit of the Spirit is love, joy, peace, patience, kindness, goodness, faithfulness, gentleness and self-control. Against such things there is no law."* Challenge your group members to memorize these verses. Then talk together about what we can do to cooperate with the Gardener—Jesus Christ—so that we will be fruitful in these ways. You might also ask group members to identify which fruit they would most like to see in their life.

DISCIPLESHIP

RPM Reduction

Spend some time talking about the challenge of living in our fast-paced world and how close it is—or isn't—to God's intentions for us. Together make a list of specific and practical ways group members can slow down their lives (i.e., obey the speed limit, choose to wait in the longest line, walk somewhere rather than drive, say "no" to another commitment, set an appointment to be with the Lord and honor it as you would any other appointment, etc.). Have each group member choose one suggestion to implement this week. You might follow up at the next meeting with a discussion of their experiences.

DISCIPLESHIP

I'd Like to Be Remembered for . . .

Take a few minutes to tell about someone you were close to who died. What do you remember most about that person? What characterized his or her life?

Then pass out a piece of paper to everyone in the group and have each of them draw a headstone on it. Next, ask them to write down their answer to the following question: What do you want your headstone to say? Encourage them to spend some quiet time with the Lord in order to determine whether they are on a path that will help them deserve that tribute, and what course corrections might be appropriate.

DISCIPLESHIP

Board of Advisors

Proverbs 15:22 (NLT) says, *"Plans go wrong for lack of advice; many counselors bring success."* Each of us needs a board of advisors to help us navigate life. Pass out a piece of paper to each group member. Have them list the names of people they would like to have on their Board of Advisors. Then discuss the following question: What would it actually take to cultivate such a board?

DISCIPLESHIP

What's in a Name?

Revelation 2:17 (NLT) says, *"I will give to each one a white stone, and on the stone will be engraved a new name that no one knows except the one who receives it."* Have each person share the meaning on their name. Talk about the significance of names in the Bible. Pass out a stone to each person in the group that they can carry in their pocket or purse as a reminder that they belong to God.

DISCIPLESHIP

Game Ball

When someone has an exceptional performance in a championship game, that person receives the game ball signed by everyone on the team. Adapt that to your small group. Simply bring a baseball or softball to your group meeting. Award this game ball to a group member you especially want to encourage. Have everyone in the group write a word of encouragement on the ball.

DISCIPLESHIP

Are You Mary or Martha?

Take time during a group meeting to read Luke 10:38–42, a brief but powerful story about two of Jesus' closest friends, Martha and Mary. Ask your group members which of the two women each of them most relates to and why. Also discuss what it means in practical terms to sit at the feet of Jesus today in the twenty-first century.

DISCIPLESHIP

Pardon Me

Read Ephesians 4:32 (NIV) to your group: *"Be kind and compassionate to one another, forgiving each other, just as in Christ God forgave you."* Then pass out a piece of paper to group members and ask them to do one of two things. 1) Write a letter of pardon and forgiveness to someone who has hurt them. Let them know that they don't have to share the letter with anyone and that this letter isn't intended to be mailed. Rather, this issue of forgiveness is between them and God. 2) If people can't think of someone they need to forgive, have them write a letter of thanks to God for forgiving their sins. This second option might even be preceded by a time of silent confession.

DISCIPLESHIP

Spiritual Stop Signs

Bring a picture of a stop sign to your group meeting. Have people talk about a time in their life when they stopped growing spiritually. What caused the stoppage? What happened to get them growing again?

DISCIPLESHIP

An Encouraging Word

Hebrews 3:13 (NIV) says, *"Encourage one another daily, as long as it is called Today, so that none of you may be hardened by sin's deceitfulness."* Read this verse to your group, emphasizing the phrase "encourage one another daily." Then challenge the people in your group to find a day in the coming week when they can encourage 20 different people. Talk about the experience at your next meeting.

DISCIPLESHIP

Passing the Baton

Read 2 Timothy 2:2 (NIV) to the group: *"The things you have heard me say in the presence of many witnesses entrust to reliable men who will also be qualified to teach others."* Then ask the following questions. 1) Who has been a significant Bible teacher or special personal mentor to you? What are one or two things that you learned from that person? 2) Who in your life might God want you to be mentoring? What truths, insights, and knowledge do you want to pass along?

DISCIPLESHIP

Unity Builders

Talk with your small group about the unity of your church. Is there true unity within your church? Have members explain why they answered as they did. Also consider whether your group is proactively promoting unity within the church. List some ways that your group can foster unity—and perhaps even community— within your church family.

DISCIPLESHIP

Invisible but Real

Bring a piece of poster board to your group meeting. Do the following brainstorming exercise with the entire group. Make a list of words that describe what the Bible says happens to a person who comes to Christ. To get the exercise started, you might begin with a few phrases like "forgiven," "justified," "reconciled," "indwelt by the Holy Spirit" . . .

DISCIPLESHIP

Problem Solvers

Take a Band-Aid®, a knife, and a toy gun to your group meeting. Ask people to identify which object best represents their approach to conflict. A Band-Aid offers a quick and superficial solution. A knife (think "scalpel") symbolizes the willingness to be honest and the ability to deal with conflict in a healthy way. The gun, however, stands for wounding people, if not totally blowing them away. Then discuss what the Bible teaches about how to deal with conflict. Close this exercise with a time of prayer for your group. Ask God to help each of you learn to handle conflict in a healthy—or healthier—manner.

DISCIPLESHIP

Spiritual Workouts

Bring some gym clothes or a gym bag to your group meeting and read 1 Timothy 4:7 (NIV)—*"Train yourself to be godly."* Then discuss the following question: In what ways is following Christ like working out at the gym?

DISCIPLESHIP

Make it Personal

Make sure everyone in the group has a Bible. Have them find Psalm 23. Ask for several volunteers to each read the Psalm slowly and aloud. Each time they come to a personal pronoun have them say their name. For example, "The Lord is JOHN'S shepherd . . ." After the Psalm has been read several times ask people which verse most speaks to them.

DISCIPLESHIP

White Noise

Turn on the television or radio during your group meeting. Every few minutes have someone inconspicuously turn up the volume a little bit. When the noise is clearly distracting, turn it off and talk about those things that easily distract us and keep us from hearing God.

DISCIPLESHIP

A Picture is Worth 1,000 Words

Bring a stack of old magazines to your group meeting. Ask people to thumb through the magazines and pull out two or three pictures that best portray their spiritual journey over the last year. Ask them to explain their selection of pictures. Finally, have each person find one picture that would best depict what they want to see happen in their spiritual life in the coming year.

MINISTRY

MINISTRY

Bless the Servants

As a group, list people who serve in your church. You might want to group them by ministry. Then spend some time praying for these faithful servants. Afterwards, ask each group member to choose one or two different people from the list and write them a note of encouragement on behalf of your group. Provide paper and pens so that the note writing definitely happens!

MINISTRY

Served by the King

Read Philippians 2:5–11. Let that passage help the group list the various ways Jesus has served us. Then spend some time finding other verses that describe the things Jesus has done for us. Close this exercise with a time of thanksgiving prayer for all that Christ our Servant-King has done for us.

MINISTRY

Servant Search

Take some extra Bibles to your group meeting so that everyone in the group will have a Bible. Have your group open their Bibles to the gospels. (You might even assign a different group to each of the four gospels.) List together all the times that Jesus modeled servanthood. Take time to read some passages aloud. Close with a discussion of what we can do to be servants in our home, church, place of business, and neighborhood.

MINISTRY

Consumer vs. Contributor

Talk about the difference between consumers and contributors. Then ask, "What evidence of a consumer mindset do you find in the church in general today—and why is this mindset an appealing option?" In contrast to that consumerism, point out some people in your church who are servant-contributors to God's kingdom work. Close by asking people to prayerfully consider the ways in which they are consumers at church and ways they could be more effective (not busier!) servant-contributors.

MINISTRY

Get Your Hands Dirty

A servant does whatever needs to be done. So talk to your group about taking on some as-yet-unspecified project at your church that no one else really wants to do. After the group has agreed to get their hands dirty, contact your pastor or a staff member to find out what project your group could do around the church that no one else wants to do. Depending on the project, this could be a great opportunity to involve your kids in ministry as well.

MINISTRY

Dream a Little

This great faith-building exercise will also give you a clue into people's passions and shapes for ministry. Simply discuss the following questions: If neither time nor money were an obstacle, what would you attempt for God? What can you do to start moving in that direction of ministry?

MINISTRY

Secret Service

Matthew 6:1–4 (NIV) says, *"Be careful not to do your 'acts of righteousness' before men, to be seen by them. If you do, you will have no reward from your Father in heaven. So when you give to the needy, do not announce it with trumpets, as the hypocrites do in the synagogues and on the streets, to be honored by men. I tell you the truth, they have received their reward in full. But when you give to the needy, do not let your left hand know what your right hand is doing, so that your giving may be in secret. Then your Father, who sees what is done in secret, will reward you."* Ask each person to respond to Jesus' teaching by accepting the challenge to anonymously meet a need in the coming week.

MINISTRY

Good Neighbors

Which group member has a neighbor with a need? Perhaps the yard could use work, some baby-sitting would be helpful, or the car could be washed and waxed. Meet that need, whatever it is—and be sure to take along some cookies or brownies when you put your love into action.

MINISTRY

Body Parts

Read 1 Corinthians 12:12–26. How well does your group function as a body? What could you do to improve your teamwork? What role can and does the Holy Spirit play in the functioning of the body of Christ? Also discuss which part of the body of Christ different people in the group represent. For example, if Mary is a good listener, she would be an ear in the body of Christ.

MINISTRY

Unseen but Not Unknown

In 1 Corinthians 12:18 (NLT) we read, *"But God made our bodies with many parts, and he has put each part just where he wants it."* And every single person who is part of the body of Christ is important.

Have your group select a person who works faithfully behind the scenes in your church. Write notes of encouragement letting that person know that even though his or her service is often unseen, it does not go unnoticed by you or, more importantly, by God.

MINISTRY

Bless Another Church

Choose another church in your town to pray for—and then pray! Intercede for the pastor(s), the ministries, and the members and friends of that church. Then have group members sign a card letting the pastor know that your group spent some time praying for his church. What an encouragement that card will be!

MINISTRY

Single-Parent Support

Support a single parent in your church or community by . . . offering to baby-sit, taking the kids to McDonald's, doing the grocery shopping, changing the oil in the car, sprucing up the yard, or delivering a meal. And, of course, pray for that family!

MINISTRY

Eye to Eye

At the close of a meeting, challenge your group to learn how to see people as Jesus sees them. Encourage members to look people in the eye this week and, as much as possible, every time they do so, to remind themselves that this person is created in the image of God and matters to God.

MINISTRY

Service with a Smile

Some of the strongest evidence of our love for Christ is our ability to love those who aren't easy to love. Jesus said in Luke 6:27 (Msg), *"To you who are ready for the truth, I say this: Love your enemies. Let them bring out the best in you, not the worst."* Ask your group members to think of someone who annoys or irritates them and then accept Christ's challenge to serve that person in love this week.

MINISTRY

Going Through the Roof for a Friend

Read the story in Mark 2:1–5 about the men who lowered their friend through the roof in order to get him to Jesus. Put a mat or towel in the middle of the circle. Ask anyone who has a need to kneel on the mat so that other group members can pray for him or her. In this way you can symbolically carry your friends to the feet of Jesus to receive healing and hope.

MINISTRY

Ministry God Notices

James 1:27 (NLT) says, *"Pure and lasting religion in the sight of God our Father means that we must care for orphans and widows in their troubles, and refuse to let the world corrupt us."* Identify a widow in your church and have someone from the group give her a call. Find out what need your group can take care of for her. Also let her know that your group will be praying for her.

MINISTRY

Serving Uncle Sam

Use connections in your small group or the larger church family to find the name and address of someone serving in the military. Then be creative as you put together a care package to send to that person. Be sure to include a note letting that person know that you are praying for him or her. Also, if that person is separated from family, consider serving the family in some way as well.

MINISTRY

Operation Christmas Child

Samaritan's Purse has developed a very simple but very powerful way to bless less fortunate children around the world. Just fill a shoebox with basic necessities and little gifts for boys and girls, ages 0–4, 5–9, and 10–14. Involve your children. Let them go shopping to fill a shoebox for someone their age. For more information, contact www.samaritanspurse.org.

MINISTRY

Bless the Children

Contact the leader of the children's Sunday-school program at your church. Arrange for your group to help out with the children's classes sometime. Serve in whatever ways the leaders need. Also, find some way to thank and honor the children's Sunday-school teachers.

MINISTRY

Ministry Meals

Who at your church is going through a crisis? Have the group prepare a meal for that person or family. When you deliver the meal, be sure to pray with and for the situation and the people involved. Your presence and your prayers may mean more than you will ever know. Also, ask someone from the group to follow up with a phone call a few days after your visit to see how the family is doing.

MINISTRY

We Love Teachers

Plan a teacher-appreciation celebration at a local elementary school. You might thank all the teachers or focus on the teachers from one specific grade. Bake cookies for the teachers and write notes of appreciation for their commitment and hard work.

MINISTRY

Servant's Towel

In a true demonstration of his servanthood, Jesus picked up a towel and washed the feet of his disciples (John 13). Recognize the Christlike service of someone in your group with a "servant's towel" award. Buy a nice, decorative hand towel to give as this award. If you want to make the award extra special, you could mount it in a shadow box and present it at a group meeting.

MINISTRY

A Surprise Birthday!

Randomly select someone in your group and throw that person a surprise birthday party even if the real birthday isn't for another four months! Let everyone in your group contribute to the festivities with food or paper goods and ask each person to bring an inexpensive, fun gift for the birthday boy or girl.

MINISTRY

Community Service

God wants your group to be salt and light in your community. So, as a ministry project, select someone in local government whom your group could serve in some way. What could you do to bless and encourage a firefighter, a police officer, or the mayor? You might take a plate of cookies to the fire station near your house.

MINISTRY

I See in You . . .

Pass out a piece of paper to everyone at your group meeting. Have them write down the name of all the other group members and, next to each name, one or two of the gifts and talents they see in that person. After people have completed their lists, go around the circle one by one and have everyone say what gifts they see in each other. This time will be a real encouragement to those involved.

MINISTRY

Double Blessings for a Single

During the Christmas season, adopt the children of a single parent. Take the kids shopping for a gift for Mom or Dad, treat them to lunch, and help them wrap the present they chose. You might also consider treating the parent to a movie pass or a restaurant gift certificate to use while you have the kids. But time without the kids just may be gift enough!

MINISTRY

Serving by Praying

Have someone from your group contact your pastor or a member of the church staff and ask for prayer requests that your group could pray for over the next month. Pass out a list of these requests to each member so that the group can pray during the week. Be sure to pray about some of these concerns at your group meeting as well.

MINISTRY

Seasoned Saints

Invite to a meeting an individual or a couple who have walked with the Lord for many years. Let your guests know that you'd like them to share stories from their life as well as wisdom about the walk of faith. In what ways have they seen the world change during their lifetime? How did they come to know Christ? What lessons or advice about the Christian life can they pass on? To make the time extra special, plan to share dinner or dessert.

MINISTRY

Pastor Appreciation

Your pastor carries the weighty responsibility of leading and caring for your church. So, during Pastor Appreciation Month in October, find a tangible way to show your pastor that you appreciate him. If your pastor is married, be sure to include his wife in your gift of appreciation. She plays a very significant role as a partner in his ministry.

MINISTRY

Fan the Flame

At one group meeting, gather around a fireplace or, if the weather allows, an outside fire pit. Read 2 Timothy 1:6 (NLT) aloud: *"This is why I remind you to fan into flames the spiritual gift God gave you when I laid my hands on you."* Discuss what it means to "fan into flames the spiritual gift God gave you." Help group members identify their gifts and talk about what can be done to "fan those gifts into flame."

MINISTRY

Car Ministry

Find a single mom or an elderly widow and take her car in for an oil change. While you have the car, check the air in the tires and the fluid levels. Before returning the car, thoroughly wash the outside and clean the inside. You might even fill up the gas tank!

MINISTRY

Service for a Season

What older couple in your church could use some help around the house when the seasons change? That assistance might be raking the leaves in their yard, cleaning out rain gutters, touching up some paint, or making sure the sprinklers work.

MINISTRY

Handle with Care

Have someone from your group contact the person in charge of the church nursery and offer your group as volunteers to work in the nursery some weekend. Your group may need some minimal training or instructions to do so, but your effort will be worth it. Also, as you work in the nursery, take a few moments to pray for each baby and his or her parents.

MINISTRY

Make a Joyful Noise

During the Christmas season, Christmas caroling can be a ministry. Find out where some older people in your church live and go caroling in their neighborhood. You could also carol in a nursing home or assisted-living facility. Christmas caroling is a great activity to do with some other small groups—and be sure to include the kids. After caroling, go to someone's house for hot chocolate and cookies.

MINISTRY

A Breakfast Surprise

Who in your group is *not* a morning person? (That shouldn't be hard to determine!) Plan a breakfast kidnapping in that person's honor. Make sure that other people in the house know you are coming. Pick up the honoree early (5:00 in the morning?). Let him or her throw on a bathrobe or some sweats, and then head out to breakfast. While you're eating, have the people in the group share what they love about this night owl. And, by the way, since you got your friend out of bed, be sure to buy his or her breakfast.

MINISTRY

Ministry on the Road

Traveling presents great opportunities for ministry. So challenge members of your group to do a little ministry when they next head out of town. One simple act is to pack a copy of *The Purpose Driven Life.* Then, as you go about your business activities or vacation fun, ask God to show you whom to give the book to before you return home. Be sure to have people report on their experiences.

MINISTRY

Shopping Ministry

One of the many challenges single parents face during the Christmas season is finding time to go shopping for their kids. So offer to baby-sit the children of a single parent so that he or she can do just that. While you have the children, do something fun with them.

MINISTRY

Acts of Compassion

Acts 4:32 (NLT) says, *"All the believers were of one heart and mind, and they felt that what they owned was not their own; they shared everything they had."* We are called to share with those around us. Meet a need of someone in your small group—cut their lawn, take them a meal, offer to baby-sit . . .

MINISTRY

Ministry of Comfort

When someone in your church passes away, reach out to the grieving family. Have group members take meals or send flowers. Also, ask everyone in the group to write a personal note in a sympathy card. Most important of all, be sure to pray for this family.

MINISTRY

Celebrate Life

When your group knows someone who has had a baby, put together a "New Baby Kit." Be creative as you fill a basket with fun items as well as essentials. Ask each person in your group to write one piece of advice on a card. It might also be a blessing to the family if your group personally delivered the baby kit (be sure to call first!). If a visit would be appreciated, be sure to pray for Mom and Dad as well as the baby while you're there. And a nice touch would be taking a simple meal for the new parents to enjoy!

MINISTRY

Marriage Ministry

When someone in your church gets married, send a card. Include each group member's best advice for developing a healthy, God-centered marriage.

If you know of a couple that has been married 50 years or longer, write them a note of appreciation. Let them know what a model and testimony their marriage is for those around them.

MINISTRY

The Great Giveaway

First Timothy 6:18 (NIV) says, *"Command [believers] to do good, to be rich in good deeds, and to be generous and willing to share."* Talk together about the fact that we have been blessed in order to be a blessing to others. In light of that fact, challenge group members to give something valuable to someone who needs it. Make it clear: We're not just giving away something that's collecting dust in our garage; we're giving away our best. The Lord can use such gracious generosity to open people's hearts and minds to him.

MINISTRY

Students in Service

Have someone from your group contact the person in charge of your church's student ministry. Work with that person to coordinate a night when some of the high-school students could baby-sit for some of the church's young families. Ask the students to do this as a ministry and to offer their service free of charge. Make sure that your group expresses appreciation in some tangible way to the students who help.

MINISTRY

Pleasing our Heavenly Dad

Watch the scene from the movie *Chariots of Fire* where Eric Liddell says, "When I run, I feel God's pleasure." Then ask your group members, "What activity gives you a sense of God's pleasure? How can you make time to do it more often?"

MINISTRY

How Your Past Can Be a Present

Start the group discussion by asking, "What experiences from your past could God use in ministry?" Talk about how God can use our most painful experiences to minister to others. If possible, give a brief example illustrating that reality. Have the group make note of any ministry ideas that arise during your discussion, and then make plans to act on them.

MINISTRY

Caring for the Poor

Jeremiah 22:16 (NIV) says, *"'He defended the cause of the poor and needy, and so all went well. Is that not what it means to know me?' declares the Lord."* Who are the poor in your community? What is your church doing to help meet their needs? Take up a spontaneous offering from your group that you will give to a ministry that helps the poor in your community.

MINISTRY

Extra-Mile Service

Read Luke 17:7–10 to your group.
What does this passage teach about being a
servant of Jesus? This week, at home or at
work, be a servant of Jesus and go the extra
mile in serving someone. At the next group
meeting, give people the opportunity to talk
about their extra-mile servant experiences.

MINISTRY

Serving Our Wives

This is a project for small groups made up of married couples. For Valentine's Day or a special non-occasion, have the husbands cook a meal and serve their wives. Guys, go all out for this occasion. Light candles, buy flowers, and use nice dishes. During the meal, have each of the men affirm their love for their wives. And, yes, men, you get to clean up after the meal.

MINISTRY

Christmas with a Cause

What family in your church or neighborhood could use your help in giving their kids a nice Christmas? Ask everyone in the group to use the money they would spend on one gift and instead buy a gift for someone in the family you have adopted. Make the parents the heroes by letting the gifts come from the mom and dad, not from your group.

MINISTRY

Coaching Kids

This is a wonderful exercise for group members who have teenage kids. Let the women take the young women out to dinner and the men do the same with the boys. Choose nice restaurants that are quiet enough for good conversation. Before the meal ends, have the adults speak a blessing over each of the children and perhaps even share a piece of godly advice about becoming an adult.

EVANGELISM

EVANGELISM

Why Ask Why?

Read Matthew 28:19 and talk about the fact that evangelism is the only one of the five purposes that you cannot do in heaven. Remind your group about this fact, discuss its implications, and encourage group members to obey this God-given command.

EVANGELISM

Hit List

Take construction paper, scissors, and markers to a group meeting. Ask everyone to develop a list of friends who need to know Christ. Then have them use the supplies you brought to make a Bible bookmark that will remind them to pray for the people whose names they write down.

From time-to-time in the weeks that follow, encourage group members to use their reminders and pray for those people on their list. Once every month or so, you might ask members to report on any new interest in spiritual things or even a new commitment to Christ made by the people they listed.

EVANGELISM

Are You Ready for Some Football?

Monday Night Football is a great opportunity to start a men's seeker group! Enjoy the games together and then, when the season is over, keep meeting, but for a different purpose. (In the aftermath of the season, you may find yourself leading a grief recovery group!). Build on the bonds formed during football games and continue to meet and nurture these relationships.

Even before football season is over, you might invite the wives to join the meetings. If they join during the season, they may want to watch the game, or they may want to do something else until after the play-offs. If the wives enjoy the football, they might cheer with the men, but after the season they could form a women's group that meets at the same time the men's group does.

EVANGELISM

Church Chat

Give each member several 3x5 cards. Then ask group members to write—one per card—an overused or trite church word or phrase. (*Salvation, fellowship,* and *share* are examples.) On the other side of the card, have the group members use different, plain-English, non-churchy terms to define these concepts. Practice talking about your faith to each other using these alternative words or phrases. You might consider implementing some kind of reward system to encourage members to avoid church chat. (Maybe a roll of Lifesavers would be appropriate!) The goal of this exercise is to help us develop vocabulary that clearly communicates to our unchurched friends.

EVANGELISM

Back-to-School Baby-Sitting Co-op

Organize group members to watch each other's kids as well as the kids of those moms you know who don't yet know Jesus as their Savior and Lord. This baby-sitting frees a group member to go shopping with her pre-Christian friend.

EVANGELISM

Christmas Caroling

Let your house be home base. Provide hot chocolate, cider, cookies, and song sheets and enjoy an evening spreading Christmas cheer throughout your neighborhood. You might consider taking along a portable stereo so that you'll have musical accompaniment and probably a better sound! When you wish people "Merry Christmas," let them know that you are a church group that meets in the neighborhood. You might also invite them to attend your church's Christmas services!

EVANGELISM

Sub-group

During your group meeting, sub-group into groups of three or four people. This fulfills two goals. First, when you sub-group consistently, you are forming a nucleus of people who could eventually start a new group. Second, subgrouping identifies potential leaders.

EVANGELISM

7 for 7

Challenge your group to be "7 for 7." For the next seven days until the group meets again, have each member pray for every seeker they have on their list. Ask God to open their minds and soften their hearts to hear and receive his truth and be saved.

EVANGELISM

1·1·1

At one o'clock, pray for one minute for one seeker on your list.

EVANGELISM

No Se Habla Ingles

If your group is especially focused on evangelism, take time off from Bible study and instead take a self-study course in English as a second language. This is an excellent way to prepare yourselves to meet a real need, to build relationships with nonbelievers, and to eventually have an opportunity to share the gospel with people from another culture.

EVANGELISM

Seeker Night

Plan a special small group meeting that is designed with seekers in mind (friends of yours who are open to the gospel and seeking the Truth). You'll definitely want to think outside the small group box in order to help a seeker feel at home. Work hard to create a comfortable, no-pressure environment.

EVANGELISM

Whom Will You Lead?

Who will follow you to heaven because you were the only Bible they read? By God's grace, that can and does happen! So who in your life comes to mind when you hear that question? For whom might you be a living Bible? Pray for the people whose names group members share.

EVANGELISM

Feeling Stumped

It's really okay to say "I don't know" to people you are witnessing to or talking with in your small group. If you don't know the answer to a question, tell the one asking, "Good question! I'm guessing that, in the last two thousand years, someone has asked that question, and I'll try to find the answer for you." If no one in the group knows the answer, ask for a volunteer to research the answer. If no one offers, do the research yourself and get back to the group and/or the seeker the following week.

EVANGELISM

Jesus Died for the EGRs, Too!

Does anyone in your group fall into the EGR (Extra Grace Required) category? That's not unusual. When you're dealing with EGR people, it's important to remember that Jesus Christ hung on the cross for them. Focusing on this truth will give you more patience for going the extra mile for the EGRs—especially if they are seekers!

EVANGELISM

Who's That Chair For?

An empty chair can communicate an important message to members during your small group meetings. That chair can remind people that God has someone new for the group. Who is that new person? Have your group pray consistently, as well as actively recruit new people who need God, love, and fellowship.

EVANGELISM

A Billboard in My Group?

There's another way that empty chair can serve as a reminder that God is putting your small group together. Set on it a piece of poster board that has written on it all the names of people you are praying for. Let the list prompt you to pray faithfully.

EVANGELISM

Work Party

Find a family in the community who needs some work done on their home. Gather for a Saturday work party and help with yard work, housecleaning, or painting. Have someone in the group (or someone from another group) bring lunch over for you and the host family to enjoy together. (You may want to work just in the morning and call it a day after lunch.) Explain that this project is an act of love from your small group and church.

EVANGELISM

Closet Night

Encourage your group members to reach deep into their closets and dig out those old outfits they no longer wear. Tell them not to feel sorry for that sweater from Aunt Gertrude; and stop fooling yourself—you'll never fit into that ten-year-old suit again! The general rule of thumb is this: if you haven't worn it in a year, then you probably won't miss it when it's gone. Ask everyone to bring their bags of clothes to your next small group meeting. During your study time, read Matthew 25:35–40, and talk about caring for the poor and living a simpler lifestyle. Before the group leaves, recruit a volunteer to take the clothes to the Salvation Army or some other worthy charity.

EVANGELISM

Barbecue Friends

Invite some seeker friends (possibly those on your Hit List, page 164) to enjoy a barbecue with your group. Encourage each group member to invite at least one friend. Keep the time together light and fun. Make sure to be sensitive to them as you plan your evening. This would probably not be the time, for instance, for thirty minutes of prayer!

Your guests will undoubtedly notice your camaraderie and perhaps be curious about your group. If they seem interested, invite them to check out the group at the next meeting.

EVANGELISM

Group Garage Sale

To help simplify your life and to raise money either for a missions project or a need in your group, church, or community, organize a garage sale. Advertise what your purpose is. For example, "Garage Sale to Benefit Habitat for Humanity. Five Families Working Together to Make a Difference."

EVANGELISM

Neighborhood Easter Egg Hunt

Invite your neighbors and friends and their children to an Easter egg hunt at a group member's home. Serve some light refreshments and let the kids go hunting. Make sure you have plenty of extra eggs (not hidden) for those saddened children who don't find as many eggs as other hunters do. Keep the time short, fun, and focused: "We are a group of Christians celebrating new life in Christ this Easter season. Thanks for joining us."

EVANGELISM

Rich Christians in a Hungry World

Read *Rich Christians in an Age of Hunger* by Ron Sider (Word Publishing), and discuss how to use material resources to benefit people in need. Consider incorporating one or more of Ron's ideas into your lifestyle. Your small group can offer one another accountability and encouragement.

EVANGELISM

Sponsor a Child

Your group can reach around the world with Christ's love by sponsoring a child in a developing country. Your monthly support will provide the child with food, clothing, and education. As a group, take time to pray for and write letters to the child as well. Contact World Vision at www.worldvision.org or Compassion International at www.compassion.com for more information.

EVANGELISM

Building Bridges

If your group is made up of a single ethnic group and you want to connect with other ethnic groups, consider inviting people from another church or people of a different ethnic origin. Have them visit a meeting and then, if theirs is an organized group, attend one of their activities. Consider a service project that you can do together.

EVANGELISM

Planet Care

We human beings have a God-given responsibility to take care of the earth (Genesis 1–2). Spend some time talking about what that stewardship assignment means. Then, to put into practice what you've learned, be good stewards of the planet by doing one of the following projects: pick up litter along a highway or in a park; plant a group garden and share in the work as well as in the produce; start compost by recycling vegetable wastes (rinds, peels, pulp, and seeds); or recycle newspapers, paper, plastic, and aluminum and use the cash for a mission project.

EVANGELISM

Global Link

Choose a foreign missionary who has Internet access. Arrange for your group to have a cyberspace chat with that person. Use an actual chat room or, if you're both on AOL, your "Buddy List" to communicate with each other. Instant messaging may be another option. Whatever technology you choose, be sure to pray for your missionary before—and even after—you sign off.

EVANGELISM

Pit Crew

If it's not practical for you to volunteer to change tires at the Indy 500, try instead to meet the needs of a missionary family who is home for a pit stop. Consider helping them recharge by providing wheels (loaning them a car); refreshment (invite them to dinner or take them meals); and encouragement (ask them to visit your group, have them talk about their ministry, and pray for them). Give 'em a "brake"—as in a break from the kids. And be sure to refuel them by meeting a specific physical or financial need.

EVANGELISM

Building for Jesus

Volunteer to build homes for the needy and the homeless. Do this in your area on Saturdays, or coordinate vacations with one another and take a week to build a home together. Contact Habitat for Humanity at 419 W. Church St., Americus, GA, 31709, or visit their website at www.habitat.org for project sites near you.

EVANGELISM

International Students Welcome

In America, we don't have to be missionaries to a foreign country in order to reach another culture. Other cultures often come to us! Contact a local college to find out if an international student needs a host home. Offer as a group to host a "Welcome to our community" social for international students in the fall. If it goes well, you might consider having another open house at Christmas and during other breaks. Most international students don't return home for the holidays. They are lonely and eager to make new friends.

EVANGELISM

A Thanksgiving Feast with Spirit

Prepare a traditional turkey meal together and invite people who don't have a place to go for Thanksgiving: international students, single people without family nearby, and people new to the community.

For a variation on this theme, prepare a meal for people in need—people in a homeless shelter, people at a rescue mission, or people in transit at a bus station. But consider preparing the meal on a day other than Thanksgiving. Many organizations offer food on that one day, but those folks still need to eat on the other 364 days of the year.

EVANGELISM

Remember When?

At one meeting have everyone tell *how* they got connected to the church or plugged into the small group, and *who* was instrumental in those decisions. Use these shared stories to remind people once again of the power of the invitation.

EVANGELISM

Mission Accomplished?

Help your small group put together a mission statement for your group so that everyone knows and remembers the purpose of meeting together.

EVANGELISM

Let's Celebrate

When your small group gives birth to a new small group, celebrate that momentous occasion with a "sending-out" party for the new host. A party needs food and fun, but this particular party also needs prayer. (Sometime down the road, have a reunion with all the second-generation small groups.)

EVANGELISM

Cans of Compassion

Matthew 25:35 (NIV) says, *"For I was hungry and you gave me something to eat, I was thirsty and you gave me something to drink, I was a stranger and you invited me in."* We are called to share with those around us. One simple way we can do that is by sharing food. Hunger is a real problem and one that your group can help meet. So, do a small group food drive. Have everyone bring some canned goods that could be donated to a shelter.

EVANGELISM

Map Your Neighborhood

Draw the street where you live and at least ten houses on your block. List on each house the names of the people who live there, including the children. Then note each family's "spiritual address": Where are they with the Lord? When you've finished, use this map as a prayer list. By the way, if this exercise helps you realize that you don't know the people who live around you, start introducing yourself and inviting people to your house for dinner!

EVANGELISM

It's Okay to Party!

Host a Matthew Party! We read in Matthew 9:10–13 that Jesus hung out with "sinners" and had dinner with them, so why can't we? One of the best ways to build relationships with nonbelievers is over a meal, especially if you are buying!

EVANGELISM

It's Nice to Share . . . Jesus

You don't have to be a "Bible thumper" to share what you know of Jesus. Simply find ways to talk to people about times God has helped you or ways that you depend on him each day. Small group members can hold one another accountable to do this kind of sharing.

EVANGELISM

Adopt a UPG

Have your group go to www.peoplegroups.org and select one of the world's unreached people groups to pray for at each meeting—and in between.

Learn what you can about the people group, where they live, how they live, and what efforts are being made to reach them with the gospel. Who knows? God may use these times of prayer to call a group member to go and minister to these people!

EVANGELISM

Prayer to Go

Whenever you talk with neighbors, ask before you leave if there is anything they would like you to pray for. If they mention something, you could even pray right then. People rarely reject prayers. Note how this effort transforms relationships even—or especially—with nonbelievers.

EVANGELISM

A Christmas Day Tradition

Most people spend Christmas afternoon sitting around reflecting on all that transpired earlier that morning and the night before. Why not start a new family tradition? On Christmas afternoon visit people in a nursing home! It can be a family or small group activity. Check out www.goodnewsministry.net for more info and other great ideas.

EVANGELISM

The Three Minute Version Please

Your small group members have probably already shared their testimonies with one another. But are they ready to share this life message with a nonbeliever who might ask, "Why are you a Christian?" Ask group members to develop a three-minute and a seven-minute version of their story and to practice telling it in the group.

EVANGELISM

Target Someone

Ask every member in your group to share only the name of one person they are in relationship with who needs Christ. Then challenge group members to spend some time in the next week with the person they mentioned. This is a great excuse to get together for dinner, but a phone call counts too! The idea is not to witness (although if the opportunity arises, go for it), but to strengthen the relationship.

EVANGELISM

Walk the Talk

Have you noticed that, in the New Testament, Jesus first ministered to a person's need and then shared the gospel with that person? Look at your "hit list" of people you want to see come to Christ and start ministering to their needs. When you do so, you will have the credibility to share the gospel with them.

EVANGELISM

Heaven or Hell

Generations of people made decisions for Christ based on their desire to avoid hell and enter heaven. Today, however, the greater motivator seems to be purpose. So commit—with your group as witnesses—to ask at least one person this week the following question: "People want to make their life count for something. What do you want to do with your life?" This question just may spark a significant or life-changing conversation.

EVANGELISM

Seeker Groups for Dummies

Many people are afraid to talk other than superficially with unbelievers, but heart-to-heart conversation needn't be threatening. Start by building relationships. Regular dinner parties or movie nights are excellent ways to help people get to know one another. Men could do a monthly movie night after the kids have gone to bed. Afterwards talk about the movie—and life!—over a cup of coffee. Be ready with good questions that will foster relationship. Women might want to meet regularly for tea or a walk. Whatever you choose, be consistent, and it won't be long before your Seeker Group is off and running.

EVANGELISM

Let God Do the Talking

Read Psalm 96:2–3, 1 Peter 2:9, and 2 Timothy 2:2. Then discuss how declaring, teaching, evangelism, and praise are linked in these scriptures.

EVANGELISM

Form Letters—And What Else?

Brainstorm ways that you can help your church welcome the people God brings to you. Most churches send form letters to first, second, and third-time visitors. Figure out what you can do to add warmth to the church's contacts with the people who walk through the doors. You want them to receive more than a form letter!

EVANGELISM

Sports Page

It's very telling that every newspaper in the United States has a sports section. People are interested in sports! So if your church doesn't have a sports ministry, start one. Begin with a single sport. Have your small group take ownership of the idea and make it happen. But don't let a sports ministry become another Parks and Recreation League. Be intentional about reaching seekers.

EVANGELISM

Cults, Anyone?

Identify a major cult in your area. Ask a group member to find a speaker who can teach about the cult's beliefs. Schedule a time at church and advertise the event. Encourage people to come and learn more about the cult and how to best communicate God's truth to the people involved in it.

EVANGELISM

Transitions

People are generally more open to the gospel when they are going through times of transition. Consider giving a transition kit tailored to the specific needs of the family you're reaching out to. Put together a new home kit for people just moving into the area; a new baby kit for folks welcoming a baby into the family; or a comfort kit for people who are grieving or fighting depression after losing a loved one or being laid off from work.

WORSHIP

WORSHIP

Hands Up!

In old westerns the sheriff tells the man in the black hat to drop his gun and get his hands up in an act of surrender. We Christians often worship God with our hands up; but surrendering your heart is where yielding to Jesus as Lord begins. Living for God is a daily decision. Discuss with your group the question, "What helps you get to that place of surrendering all that you are to God?"

WORSHIP

Walk This Way

Plan a group prayer walk. Pick a route and have your group pray together as you walk. Notice your surroundings as you walk and use what you see as direction for your prayers.

WORSHIP

The Love Connection

Have each group member find a favorite verse about God's love and read it to the group. This sharing may encourage others to open up and read their Bibles, to do some research, and to interact with one another.

WORSHIP

Suppertime?

If your church allows you as a small group leader to serve the Lord's Supper, then this idea is a must. Talk about what the elements mean to each one of your group members now. Ask them to reflect on the day they turned their life over to Christ. In what ways, if any, did Communion mean something different to them then? Next, discuss the role that Communion plays in your relationship with the Lord. After a time of prayer for the gift of Communion and the sacrifice of Jesus' death on the cross, share the bread and cup together.

WORSHIP

Alphabet Prayer

For a different approach to prayer, try praising God by naming his attributes in alphabetical order. The first person, for instance, will praise God because he is A—All-powerful; the second person, because he is B—Beautiful; the third person, because he is C—Compassionate, etc.

WORSHIP

Keep a Prayer Journal

It's harder to forget God's abundant blessings and it's easier to avoid the sense that he is distant when we keep a prayer journal. After all, that sense that God is far away usually comes because, like the Israelites, we forget all that God has done in our lives and in our group's life. But writing down our prayer requests, and later noting when and how God answered our prayers, helps us remember God's faithfulness. Of course, we know that he never leaves or forsakes us, but we are forgetful creatures!

WORSHIP

A Picture of Forgiveness

Add actions to words of confession. Pass around a towel (preferably white) and have group members confess their sin by using a permanent marker to write a confession on the towel. After the towel has been passed around the circle and everyone has written on it spend some time in prayer. Then take the towel outside to a grill or a fire pit where it can be burned. Let the fire be a picture of God forgiving the sin you have confessed.

WORSHIP

Preparing for Prayer

Before moving into your prayer time, set the mood of the room by dimming the lights or softly playing some instrumental music in the background. These small acts can help the people in your small group quiet their hearts and focus on the Lord.

WORSHIP

Pass the Water, Please!

Challenge your small group to pray and to fast for a special request or crisis someone recently shared. Group members will grow closer as they fast and pray together to seek God's will. (Note: Also see special books on fasting such as *God's Chosen Fast* and *Fasting for Spiritual Breakthrough*.)

WORSHIP

It's in the Follow-Through

After hearing prayer requests and praying about them together as a group, assign group members to go to the homes of those members with special prayer requests. During the home visit, see how those members are doing, offer various kinds of support, and pray with them.

WORSHIP

An All-Nighter!

Start your group at about 9 p.m. on a Friday night. (Take the kids and have them sleep in a common room.) Have your regular group meeting. Know that without time restrictions, prayer will move at a more relaxed pace. After the study, have a midnight-snack break. Next, let each group member lead a half-hour prayer session. After that or around 5:00 a.m., whichever comes first, have a time for praise reports and then celebrate God's goodness with a group breakfast. This is an event that your kids will remember, and it will model for them a real commitment to prayer.

WORSHIP

It's a Phone-By Prayer!

This is very different from those drive-by shootings that used to happen so frequently on Los Angeles freeways!

Call someone in your group. When that person answers the phone, say, "I wanted to call and have the chance to pray for you," and then offer up a prayer to the Lord and/or encouragement to the person. Don't give your fellow group member a chance to talk to you. Just pray and get off the phone. And know that the person you dialed just experienced a "phone-by prayer!"

WORSHIP

Dealer's Choice

Write a prayer request or two on a 3x5 card. Pass the card around the circle to the third person on your left. (That enables the person sitting next to a spouse or a friend to be known by someone else in the group.) Now pray together about the concerns expressed on the cards—and know that simply reading from the card is definitely allowed!

By the way, this little card can be an excellent way to get someone into the habit of praying. Encourage group members to pray about the requests during the week and to give the writer a call before the next meeting to encourage him or her. Go to that meeting expecting to be blessed and challenged as you hear about everybody's prayer experiences and learn how God may have already answered prayers.

WORSHIP

Nerf Ball with a Twist

Did you know that a Nerf ball can add a new kind of energy to your prayer time? Share a prayer request, throw the ball to someone, and have the person who catches the ball pray for you. That person then shares a prayer request, tosses the ball, and is prayed for. You get the pattern!

Besides generating prayer, the Nerf ball approach encourages the person who catches the ball to pray. Being tossed the ball says that the recipient is trusted with what has been shared and trusted to be faithful in prayer. Tossing the Nerf ball also gives people who may not usually share a prayer request an opportunity to do just that.

WORSHIP

House Calls

During group time make a house call to a member or two who haven't been able to attend. Stop by for a few minutes, drop off some goodies, and move on. You could say, "We missed you coming to the group, so we brought the group to you!" Be sure to ask how you can pray for the person you're visiting—and pray right then!

WORSHIP

On-the-Street Interviews

Gather some video cameras and send out teams of between three and six people. Instruct them to go to different places to interview people on the street. Give them a set amount of time and ask them to bring back their videos to share with the group either that night or the following week. Here are some possible questions for the interviews: "We are from [name of church], and we have a quick question to ask you. When you hear the word *worship*, what comes to mind?" "Why do you think people worship God?" and "Why do you or don't you make worship a priority in your life?" Use the video clips to gain a fresh perspective on worship.

WORSHIP

Smelly Feet?

Host a foot-washing service on Maundy Thursday, the Thursday of Holy Week and the day we remember that Jesus washed the feet of his disciples. While you are washing someone's feet, ask if that person would like to share a prayer request—and then pray as you scrub.

WORSHIP

Under the Sky

Have your group celebrate Communion outdoors. You'll be amazed by how the different setting impacts the worship experience.

WORSHIP

Sing!

Ask group members to bring a favorite worship CD to a meeting. Take turns sharing a much-loved song. Encourage group members to either sing along or to enjoy a quiet time of worship as they follow along with the words. Never be afraid to include singing in your group time.

WORSHIP

Two for One

If your church prints music sheets to insert into the weekly bulletin, ask the music ministry to include the guitar chords above the words so that your small group can use the same songs in its worship time.

WORSHIP

Water Party

Encourage the group to attend a new believers' baptism service. It's one of life's most joyous worship opportunities. (If no one in your group is getting baptized, read the *Big Ideas* section on evangelism!) ☺

WORSHIP

Lift Your Voices!

Have your group worship and sing a cappella. Nothing compares to the sound of voices lifted to the Lord in heartfelt praise!

WORSHIP

Ancient Words of Praise

During worship time, have group members read a psalm or two and then spend some quiet minutes reflecting on the words.

WORSHIP

Worship Together!

Have your group sit together during a church service. This shared worship experience can help build unity in the group as well as offer accountability when it comes to church attendance.

WORSHIP

Pester the Pastor

Find out what your pastor or the person in charge of small groups likes to eat: What snacks, junk food, fast food, or sodas are personal favorites? Ask each person in your group to pick up one of these treats or a gift certificate and bring it to the next meeting. Plan surprise deliveries of the goodies so that the recipient gets an anonymous gift each day for a week or so from a caring small group that is praying for church leaders.

WORSHIP

The Lord Is *My* Shepherd

Have someone in the group slowly read Psalm 23 aloud, and emphasize the personal pronouns in the passage. In the first line, for example, the reader would say, "The Lord is *my* shepherd." Encourage group members to close their eyes and try to picture in their minds the rich images of these verses. Silently worship Jesus, your Shepherd!

WORSHIP

Fact Sheet

Bring a poster board to your group meeting and together list truths about God and his wonderful character traits. Then spend time in prayer praising God for who he is.

WORSHIP

Music that Ministers

Psalm 150 mentions a variety of instruments that we can use to worship God. After all, there is more than one right way to worship him.

Ask for a volunteer to read Psalm 150 aloud. Then talk about what style of music most helps people in your group connect to God. Celebrate your diversity.

WORSHIP

Praying Scripture

Ask for someone in the group to read Psalm 96 aloud. Then ask someone else in the group to read it. Finally, have the whole group read it together as a prayer to God.

WORSHIP

What's in a Name?

List all the names of God that your group can think of. Ask people in the group to say which of God's names means the most to them right now and why. Later, during your prayer time, use those names of God as you pray for one another.

WORSHIP

Cleansing Fire

Gather around a fire pit or even an outdoor grill for a brief service of confession and forgiveness. Give group members a piece of paper and ask them to write down sins they need to confess. Afterwards, have them put their list in the fire. Then read Psalm 103:8–12 (NIV) aloud: *"The Lord is compassionate and gracious, slow to anger, abounding in love. He will not always accuse, nor will he harbor his anger forever; he does not treat us as our sins deserve or repay us according to our iniquities. For as high as the heavens are above the earth, so great is his love for those who fear him; as far as the east is from the west, so far has he removed our transgressions from us."* Celebrate God's gracious and complete forgiveness of our sin.

WORSHIP

A Sunday Battle

Every week during your church's worship services, a spiritual battle rages. As your pastor preaches, people are constantly deciding whether or not they will follow God. So, some Sunday morning, find a room in the church where your small group can pray during the entire worship service. Ask the pastor ahead of time if he has anything specific for you to pray about during worship.

WORSHIP

Suffering Saints

Persecution of Christians is a reality in our world. Every single day, literally thousands of Christians take great risks to follow Jesus and spread the good news of Christ. Ask for a volunteer to read John 15:18–21 during your small group meeting. Then spend some time praying for persecuted Christians around the world.

WORSHIP

Spiritual Green Card

Before your group meeting, buy some green 3x5 cards from a local office supply store. Pass out the cards to your group. Then read Philippians 3:20 (NLT) which says *"But we are citizens of heaven, where the Lord Jesus Christ lives. And we are eagerly waiting for him to return as our Savior."* Have group members write this verse on their card. It will be their spiritual "green card" this week, a reminder that this world is not our true home. We are citizens of the kingdom of God.

WORSHIP

Confession Is Good for the Soul

Is your group ready to take a risk and experience God's forgiveness in a new way? If so, read James 5:16 (NLT) aloud to your group: *"Confess your sins to each other and pray for each other so that you may be healed. The earnest prayer of a righteous person has great power and wonderful results."* Ask group members a few questions about this verse: Why would God want us to confess our sins to one another? What are the possible benefits of doing so? When, if ever, have you confessed your sin to someone? What was that experience like? Does anyone feel prompted by the Lord to confess something to the group right now?

WORSHIP

Don't Ask

Close a meeting with a different kind of prayer time. Don't ask for a thing. Instead spend time praising and worshiping God, and offering prayers of thanksgiving.

WORSHIP

Come Home

Hear what James 5:19 (Msg) says: *"My dear friends, if you know people who have wandered off from God's truth, don't write them off. Go after them. Get them back."* Now share the names of friends and family members who have wandered from the faith. Ask God to show you any step he might want you to take to help them return to Christ.

WORSHIP

I Love My Church

The church is the body of Christ and the bride of Christ. While churches are far from perfect, God still loves his church, and so should we. As a group, make a list of things you love most about your church. Be specific. Spend time giving thanks to God for the items on your list.

WORSHIP

Get Members to Remember

Pair up with someone in the group and together memorize Romans 12:1 (NIV), one of the Bible's key verses about worship. It says, *"Therefore, I urge you, brothers, in view of God's mercy, to offer your bodies as living sacrifices, holy and pleasing to God—this is your spiritual act of worship."* At your next meeting, see how many people can quote the verse. Then talk about what it means. Be specific: What does "[offering] your bodies as living sacrifices" look like in real, twenty-first century life?

WORSHIP

Holy Odor

Bring a bottle of perfume to the group meeting. Spray the bottle in the room a few times. Read Matthew 26:6–13. Then talk together about what it would look like today to love Christ and others with a lavish, extraordinary love.

WORSHIP

Amazing Grace

Find the words to "Amazing Grace." Any church hymnal will have this song, and you can probably find the words on the Internet. At a meeting, either sing the song together, or you could read the lyrics to your group. Ask the people in your group which verse of the song means the most to them and why.

WORSHIP

Prayer Partners

At the close of your group meeting, ask the people in your group to commit to having a prayer partner for a week. You might draw names out of a hat, assign partners, or let group members pair up on their own. Ask the prayer partners to contact each other every day for prayer either in person, by phone, or via e-mail.

WORSHIP

A Different Kind of Prayer

Ask for three volunteers to read one of the following prayers of the apostle Paul: Ephesians 1:15–21; 3:14–21, and Colossians 1:9–12. Talk about the ways these prayers differ from the prayers you hear most Christians pray today. Spend some time echoing Paul's prayers as you pray for people in your group.

WORSHIP

A Great Big God

Have someone read Isaiah 40:18–31 aloud. What aspects of God's greatness does this passage celebrate? Spend some time praising God for his greatness and majesty.

WORSHIP

Favorites Night

At the end of a meeting, ask group members to bring a CD of their favorite Christian song to the next meeting. At that meeting, have members play the song they brought and then explain why that song is a current favorite.

WORSHIP

Silent, But Not Absent

Read Psalm 13 aloud to your group. When, if ever, have you felt like David did in Psalm 13? Ask volunteers to talk about times when God has seemed silent or distant. Were they able to still trust God? Why or why not? What did these people learn from their experience of God's silence?

WORSHIP

The Ultimate Worship Service

Read Revelation 5 aloud to your group. Then ask them to close their eyes and try to imagine the scene as you read the chapter a second time. What do group members find most striking about the scene? Most surprising? Most inspiring?

WORSHIP

Prayers on Paper

Sometimes it is helpful to write out prayers on paper, so ask group members to write down a prayer or two this week. Encourage them to bring these prayers with them to the next group meeting. Some people may be willing to share their prayers; others may want to talk about the experience. What was helpful or challenging or wonderful about writing out prayers?

WORSHIP

The Horizontal Impacts the Vertical

The Bible says that our relationships with people (relationships in the horizontal dimension) can impact our worship of God (our relationship in the vertical dimension). Have someone read Matthew 5:23–24 to your group. Is a group member's worship being hindered because of a relationship that needs to be reconciled? If so, pray together for the reconciliation of that relationship.

WORSHIP

Stars in Your Eyes

Some night when the sky is clear, take your group outside for a time of worship. Read Psalm 19:1–2 (NLT). Those verses say, *"The heavens tell of the glory of God. The skies display his marvelous craftsmanship. Day after day they continue to speak; night after night they make him known."* During prayer time, ask people to keep their eyes open and to look at the heavens as they, too, declare the glory of God.

ABOUT THE AUTHORS

 Steve Gladen is the Pastor of Small Groups at Saddleback Church and has been on staff since 1998. His focus has been on small groups here at Saddleback and other churches for over the past fifteen years. Steve oversees the strategic launch and development of small groups as well as the staff of the Small Group Network. Steve is passionate about seeing groups balance the five purposes in their groups and in their individual lives. He loves seeing a big church become "small" through the true community that is experienced in small groups. Steve and his wife, Lisa, have two children, Erika and Ethan, and have been married since 1989.

 Lance Witt joined the Saddleback staff as Pastor of Spiritual Maturity in 2001 after twenty years as a senior pastor in Arkansas, Texas, and New Mexico. Lance oversees the development of small group tools at Saddleback. His own journey has made him passionate about building small groups that enable people to live out the five purposes of the church. Lance also serves on the Teaching Team and is one of the Executive Pastors at Saddleback Church. Lance and his wife, Connie, have two children, Jonathan and Meagan, and have been married since 1978.

Steve and Lance are not only pastors, they are also active small group leaders. Between the two of them, they have over 32 years of small groups experience.